The Collector

A play

Mark Healy
Adapted from the novel
by John Fowles

Samuel French — London
New York - Toronto - Hollywood

THE COLLECTOR

An earlier version of this play was first performed at the
Derby Playhouse in a co-production with the Royal
Lyceum Theatre, Edinburgh, on 2nd October 1998 with
the following cast:

Frederick Clegg	Mark Letheren
Miranda Grey	Danielle Tilley

Directed by Mark Clements
Design by Steven Richardson
Lighting by Chris Ellis

CHARACTERS

Frederick Clegg, late twenties
Miranda Grey, nineteen

SYNOPSIS OF SCENES

ACT I

ACT II

ADAPTER'S NOTES

In the original production, at the end of the Prologue, Clegg opened a central wall or curtain to reveal the cellar behind. The rest of the house and playing areas were above and around the cellar. DS was the dining-room, lounge and garden. Stairs at either side of the stage led up to a landing above the cellar from which a couple of doors led off stage to unseen rooms including the bathroom. Each area was differentiated by lighting.

Steven Richardson produced an extraordinary, operatic set with scene changes marked with huge butterflies lit up behind gauze walls. As Miranda's plight became worse so the butterflies became less. Clegg stood above her on the landing watching and studying her during his speeches. It was very powerful and extravagant.

However, I originally wrote the play for an "in-the-round" space. Clegg circled a mound of props that formed the walls of a circular cellar in which Miranda was imprisoned.

The options are there for many styles of staging but essentially the cellar, the house and garden should be seperated by levels, lighting or different areas.

As with the set, the lighting and effects plot can be played with but it should be clear who we see and who the characters are talking to (themselves, the audience or each other) at every moment.

Mark Healy

Every Night and Every Morn
Some are Born to sweet delight
Some are Born to sweet delight
Some are Born to Endless Night

William Blake

ACT I

Darkness

Bach's Goldberg Variations *plays*

A video image flicks on. The film, shot from a distance and obviously home-made, shows a girl (Miranda) in different parts of London. The camera follows her going to an art college, coming out of a tube station, walking in a park, shopping, entering a pub, etc.

The Lights come up DS on Frederick Clegg. He is in his late twenties, bland-looking in bland clothes. He cradles a shoe-box in his hands. He watches the video, mumbling to himself, barely audible — "Oh yes, of course", "Nearly saw me there", "That's the best bit" etc.

After a couple of minutes of footage the film freeze-frames on the closest shot of the girl so far and this is the first time we really see her face — she is beautiful

The music fades as Clegg stares in wonder. There is a silence, then he breaks his trance-like state to take in the audience. He becomes self-conscious as he feels their eyes on him

Throughout all his narration Clegg is constantly trying to justify his actions. He is never arrogant but talks to the audience both as his confidante and ally. He takes us into his world and through the story of his obsession, in order to absolve himself. At no time can he possibly face the truth of his guilt

Clegg (*beginning nervously*) They say, "There are two sides to every story." I think that's very true. People are always jumping to the wrong conclusions, judging situations they don't really know anything about. You see, unless you were there and saw what happened, took part in it, got caught up in all the feelings, you just wouldn't understand. You couldn't. The truth is a lot more complicated. So, that's what this is all about. It's my chance to tell you what happened — from my side.

I suppose it all started when I won the money. You see, none of this would have happened without the money. I just couldn't have done any of it. I mean, I'd thought about doing it for ages — well, day-dreamed about it. For years. I've always been a bit like that, gone off on endless made-up stories about how things might be different one day. Fantasies, I suppose. But what I never imagined was that these fantasies would come true — well, some of them anyway. But I'm jumping ahead. Sorry. What's important at the beginning is that it was all just a dream, for a long time. And then, I won the money.

He looks back at the video

I can't say what it was about Miranda, but the very first time I saw her, I knew she was the only one. It was that simple. Of course, I'm not mad. I knew it was just a dream and it always would have been if it hadn't been for the money. That's my point.

When something like that happens your whole life changes, everything, and you start to think maybe your dreams can come true. Well, I left work. I didn't really know what to do at first. Suddenly, I had all the freedom in the world. What I thought I'd do was go to all the places where you can find rare species and aberrations and get proper serious. I mean turn up and stay somewhere for as long as I liked, and go out and collect and take photos. The money meant I could buy all the best equipment. I got myself a special van too. There were so many species I wanted — the Swallowtail for example, and rare fritillaries like the Heath and Glanville. Things that most collectors only get a go at once in a lifetime. There were moths too, I thought I might take them up.

It's funny, I kept on thinking I was never going to see Miranda again. I was so caught up in all the excitement and everything I really thought I might forget her. But forgetting's not something you do, it happens to you. Only it never happened to me. All that time I couldn't get her out of my head. She haunted me, as they say. I knew I could never get to know her in the ordinary way. She and her friends would never give me the time of day. But I started to think that if she was with me, just me, she'd see all my good points, she'd understand. I even tried reading proper papers and going to art galleries and museums. I didn't enjoy it much but I did it so I could talk to her, so I wouldn't seem ignorant. It wasn't really a plan, just a few things to do, to improve myself — for her.

The thing is that while I was looking through one of the papers I found this:

He takes out a scrapbook from the box, opens it up and flicks through it until he finds a newspaper cutting

So, I suppose it was fate really that started it all off. Here we are ...

"Far From the Madding Crowd? Old cottage, charming secluded surroundings, large garden, one hour by car from London, two miles from nearest village ..."

And so on. You see, I wasn't even looking for a place at all but the next morning I was driving down to see it.

I didn't come down here with the intention of seeing whether there was anywhere to have a guest. It's true, I can't really say what intention I had. (*He puts the scrapbook back and places the box at his feet to mask his confusion*) It wasn't something I planned the moment I won the money. It was a sort of series of coincidences.

Anyway, I remember the estate agent started to get all cocky — I obviously wasn't what he expected. I told him I was rich. I was even going to say it wasn't for me, not big enough, just to show him, when he said, "Do you want to see the cellar?" (*He smiles for the first time as he remembers this turning point*) It was perfect. I couldn't have hoped for better.

Even now, I wake up sometimes and it feels like it's all been a dream, like down there doesn't exist. It's like two different worlds, completely cut off from each other. Just a dream. My secret little world.

Clegg pulls back a curtain or central wall to reveal a cellar. The cellar is neatly furnished with a bed, large folding screen, wall mirror, wardrobe, table and chair, and a bookcase full of expensive art books. There is a door that leads off stage to an outer cellar

Lying on the bed is Miranda Grey; nineteen years old and beautiful. She is fully dressed, gagged and bound. Her hair is all dishevelled and sweaty. She is unconscious. Clegg stands over her and switches on the bedside lamp. He unties her

When you're in love you can do anything, it's like something inside you constantly pushing you on. "What water is to the body, purpose is to the mind", they say and I think that's very true because when Miranda became my purpose I became as good as the next man. I bought the house straight away, got some people in to do up this place — told them I was going to use it as a studio for photography. Then I went up to find Miranda. I followed her for a few days — got to know her routine — and then ... I just did it.

Clegg carefully takes off the gag

I

It was so easy really. There was a quick struggle but I got her in the van ...
That first touch — she was so light, so much smaller than I'd thought.

He stands staring at her, heart pounding

Yes, I suppose that's how it all began.

The Lights change

SCENE 1
FIRST CONVERSATION

The cellar

*Miranda comes round and is violently sick over the side of the bed. She gasps
for breath. Clegg backs away and goes behind the screen and returns with
a bucket*

Clegg (*very tentatively; this is the moment his fantasy becomes reality, for
better or worse*) Hello. How are you? I'm sorry — I didn't realize it had
that effect on people. Well, this is your room, I hope you find it comfortable.
I'm just upstairs so I'll make sure you have everything you need. There's
all sorts of books there for you and clothes. Just ask for anything you want.
Oh yes, what would you like for breakfast? I've got most things — cereal,
eggs, toast, you can even have French croissants, if you like.
Miranda Where am I?
Clegg I'm afraid I can't tell you that.
Miranda Who are you? Why have you brought me here?
Clegg Don't start worrying about all that now. Get some rest. Have some
water. It's just there, and the Ladies is just behind the screen — I'm sorry
it's so basic — I couldn't get any pipes down here. (*He turns to leave the
cellar*)
Miranda I demand to be released at once. Do you hear me? (*She moves
towards the cellar door*)

Clegg blocks her and throws her back on to the bed forcefully

Clegg You can't go yet. Please don't oblige me to use force again. (*He backs
away*) We'll talk tomorrow. Good-night.

Clegg exits from the cellar, locking the door behind him

Miranda Wait! Come back, come back!

After a pause, Miranda starts to look around the room, discovering all Clegg's preparations; the wardrobe is full of clothes her size and underwear. She continues to look as ——

Clegg enters DS outside the cellar

THE BEST THING I'VE EVER DONE

Clegg (*to the audience*) Afterwards, she was always telling me what a bad thing I had done and how I ought to try and realize it more. I can only say that when she came to stay, that first evening I was so happy, happier than I had ever been in my life. My intentions were for the best, you see, that's what she never understood. It's the best thing I've ever done. It was like catching a Mazarine Blue or a Queen of Spain Fritillary — a dream come true.

Finally, Miranda sits in absolute horror

The Lights fade to Black-out

SCENE 2
MIRANDA GREY (DAY 1)

The cellar

There is a knocking on the cellar door, followed by the sound of keys in the lock

The Lights come up on Miranda standing in the middle of the cellar

Clegg enters

Clegg Good-morning.
Miranda Where have you been? I've been waiting for ages.
Clegg I hope you slept well.
Miranda What time is it?
Clegg Just after eight.
Miranda Look, I don't know who you think I am. But if you think I'm from a rich family or something and you're going to get a lot of money, you're wrong.
Clegg (*trying to reassure her*) Oh, don't worry, I know who you are. You're Miranda Grey. You live at No. 32 Kensington Crescent but at the moment

you're studying at St Martin's School of Art in London. You won a scholarship. So you're sharing with other students in Muswell Hill. Your father's Dr Grey. You used to go to Ladymont School for girls. It's funny you trying to make out you're not rich — some would say you're very rich. But you needn't worry, it's not money.

Miranda Oh my God ...

Clegg What?

Miranda I know you, don't I?

Clegg (*completely thrown*) No.

Miranda Yes — you work at the Job Centre — I've seen you.

Clegg I don't know what you mean.

Miranda Yes, you do. You were in the paper. The Lottery, you won it. We all said we had seen you about.

Clegg panics and quickly turns to leave

Wait! Don't go! Why am I here? If you know so much about me, why have you brought me here?

Clegg (*improvising quickly*) I was forced to.

Miranda Forced to? By whom?

Clegg (*turning*) I can't tell you that.

Miranda What are you talking about? Tell me why I'm here.

Clegg I'm only obeying orders.

Miranda Whose orders?

Clegg I can't tell you.

Miranda Whose orders?

Clegg (*clutching at straws*) Mr Singleton.

Miranda What?

Clegg I'm not meant to tell you, he'd kill me if he knew.

Miranda Mr Singleton? My old headmaster?

Clegg It's not what you think.

Miranda Mr Singleton ordered you to kidnap me? Why?

Clegg I don't know.

Miranda Of course you do — why?

Clegg (*thinking quickly*) Do you remember the girl in Penshurst Road? The one that disappeared two years ago?

Miranda No ... What happened to her?

Clegg I don't know, but he did it.

Miranda Did what?

Clegg (*clumsily*) I don't know. I don't know what happened to her. But he did it ... Whatever it was. She's never been heard of since.

Miranda So Mr Singleton kidnaps girls and you help him?

Clegg nods

Why? Why do you help him?

Clegg I have to — I can't tell you. I'm not meant to tell you anything. I'm not going to answer any more questions.

Miranda What's he going to do with me?

Clegg I don't know.

Miranda Where is he now?

Clegg He'll be coming — I expect.

Miranda Of course, this must be his house in Suffolk.

Clegg Yes.

Miranda He hasn't got a house in Suffolk.

A stand off

Clegg (*trying to change the subject*) I came to ask you what you'd like for breakfast. There's cereal, eggs, toast ...

Miranda I don't want any fucking breakfast ... This bloody room and that stuff you used — what the fuck was it?

Clegg (*shocked by her language*) Chloroform. I didn't know it would make you sick. Honest.

Miranda (*sarcastically*) Mr Singleton should have told you.

Clegg (*flustered*) You must want something?

Miranda How long are you going to keep me here?

Clegg I don't know ... I mean, it's not up to me. (*Trying to regain control*) I'm going to the shops now. You must tell me what you want. I'll buy anything you need.

Miranda Anything?

Clegg Well ...

Miranda Mr Singleton told you to?

Clegg No, this is from me.

Miranda I just want to get out of here.

Clegg Well — apart from that what would you like?

Miranda Look, we're going to start all over again. I don't believe what you've said about Mr Singleton. It's ludicrous. I know his daughter, he's not like that. And if he was, he certainly wouldn't have you working for him. He wouldn't have done all this either.

Clegg cannot look at her. Miranda is almost talking to herself, trying to make sense of it all

You've gone to a lot of trouble. All those clothes in there, all these books.

They must be worth a fortune. You've locked me up, but you want me to
be comfortable here. So there are two possibilities: you're holding me for
money — you're in a gang or something.

Clegg I'm not, I've told you.

Miranda Yes, you know who I am. My father is not rich. So it can't be
money. And you don't need the money anyway. (*Daring to say it*) The only
other thing — is sex.

Clegg (*with shock*) It's not that at all. I shall have all proper respect. I'm not
that sort.

Miranda (*desperately*) Then you must be mad. What else is there?

Clegg No.

Miranda You admit that the Mr Singleton story is a lie?

Clegg I wanted to break it to you gently.

Miranda Break what? Rape? Murder?

Clegg I never said that.

Miranda Then why am I here?

Clegg (*pleading*) I can't tell you.

Miranda Why not? You attack me in the street, you drug me ——

Clegg I didn't attack you.

Miranda Yes, you did! You asked me to help with some dog! You've locked
me up and bought me all these things — all I'm asking is why! Tell me!
Just tell me why I'm ...

Clegg (*suddenly*) I love you.

Silence

(*Very awkwardly*) You're right, I work at the Job Centre, well, I used to.
And I saw you when you signed on — before you went to art college. You
came in once with your friends and that was it. I couldn't stop thinking
about you. I found out where you lived and watched your house whenever
I could, just hoping to get a glimpse. I used to take my lunch and eat it in
the park opposite. I'd see you practising the piano in your front room,
taking your dog for a walk, going for drinks. I made sure you never saw me.

Then I won the money, like you said. I knew you'd never look at me, even
with the money. I know you're not like that. But you see, I wanted to ...
I felt I would do anything to know you, to be able to — Not to spy on you
— but ... So I wanted you to be my guest — here.

*Miranda just stares at him in disbelief. Clegg's admission has changed
everything*

Miranda (*softly*) I see. And you think, by keeping me here, you'll make me
feel something for you?

Clegg I just want to get to know you.

Pause

Miranda This is insane. OK, if you love me in any real sense of the word love you can't want to keep me here. You can see that, can't you? The air in this place, I couldn't breathe last night. I woke up with a headache this morning. I'll die if you keep me locked up in here.

Clegg It won't be long, I promise.

Miranda (*trying a new warmer tack*) What's your name?

Clegg Clegg.

Miranda Your first name?

Clegg Frederick.

Miranda Do people call you Freddie — or Fred?

Clegg Always Frederick.

Miranda Look, Frederick, I'm very flattered but ... I don't know ... Perhaps we could become friends somewhere else. I — I do like gentle, kind men. But I couldn't possibly — not in this room ... I can see you're ashamed of all this, what you've done ... Aren't you?

Clegg I just want to get to know you.

Miranda (*snapping*) But you can't kidnap people just to get to know them!

Clegg I want to know you so much though. I wouldn't have a chance in London. I'm not clever like that. You wouldn't be seen dead with me.

Miranda That's not true.

Clegg I'm not blaming you.

Miranda That's rubbish, I'm not like that. Some of my best friends are like you — I mean, they're from your kind of background. (*She controls herself again*) I suppose it's in all the papers?

Clegg I haven't looked.

Miranda You could go to prison for this, you know. For years.

Clegg Be worth it. Be worth going for life.

Miranda Right, I promise ... I swear if you let me go I won't tell anyone. I'll make something up. Then we can meet up in London, just the two of us. No-one else will ever know about this.

Clegg I can't. Not now.

Miranda But if you let me go now I would admire you. I'd think, you loved me, you had me at your mercy, but you were very — fair, you behaved like a real gentleman.

Clegg I can't. Don't ask. Please don't ask.

Miranda I'd want to get to know someone like that.

Clegg (*he can't take any more*) I've got to go now.

Miranda (*very gently*) Please, Frederick.

The Lights fade on Miranda

Clegg turns and moves DS

THE PAPERS

Clegg (*to the audience*) I suppose you can't prepare for everything. I mean as Aunt Annie says, "Even the best made plans" and all that. I should have guessed she'd catch me out, I should have been more careful. I thought I'd have to go down and drive her back to London like she wanted, I could go abroad. But that was just being stupid. You see the silly thing was I had told myself a dozen times before "I mustn't tell her I love her", but let it come out naturally. No, I couldn't expect everything to be right straight away. It would take time and effort on both our parts. I was going to have to be patient.

I went into town that morning and bought all the papers. Like she said, it was all over the front page. I really couldn't believe how much stuff there was on her.

All the reports said she was pretty and they all had the same photo, with her beautiful smile. It made me realize that she hadn't smiled once since she arrived here. If she was ugly she wouldn't have got more than a couple of paragraphs.

Clegg moves into the cellar, carrying a tray, still talking to the audience. The lights come up half-state on Miranda in the cellar. This sets up the convention that Clegg can narrate his story while with and watching Miranda. Miranda takes the tray and begins to eat

I never let her see the papers though or have a radio or television. I told her I didn't see or hear any news either. It was much simpler that way.

The Lights come up fully on the cellar

SCENE 3

FIRST ESCAPE ATTEMPT AND THE ARRANGEMENT (DAY 3)

The cellar. Supper

Miranda eats some of the food then pushes it away with disdain

Clegg I haven't had much culinary experience.

Miranda Why not? How old are you? Twenty-eight?

Clegg About that.

Miranda (*sarcastically*) Oh, sorry, I didn't mean to be rude.

Clegg It's all right.

Miranda Well, I hope whoever cooks for you does better than that. Is there anyone else upstairs?

Clegg No. Before the money came I lived with my aunt and cousin. Aunt Annie did the cooking. They're not about any more.

Miranda Where are they now? In the next cellar?

Clegg (*not amused*) In Australia.

Miranda What?

Clegg I paid for them to go on a cruise. Aunt Annie's got a brother out there.

Miranda Your uncle.

Clegg Yes.

Miranda And you decided to stay here with me. I'm flattered.

Clegg Yes.

Miranda looks at him, taken aback by his honesty. Clegg turns to go

Well, I better get on with the washing-up.

Miranda No, wait. Tell me about yourself.

Clegg (*turning*) Nothing to tell really.

Miranda Tell me what you do in your spare time. You must have a lot since you won the money.

Clegg is surprised by her interest

Well?

Clegg (*proudly*) I'm an entomologist. I collect butterflies.

Miranda Yes, I remember it said in the paper. Now you've collected me.

Clegg In a manner of speaking.

Miranda No, not in a manner of speaking. Literally. You've pinned me in this little room so you can come and gloat over me whenever you want.

Clegg I don't think of it like that at all.

Miranda Do you know I'm a Buddhist? I hate anything that takes life. Any kind of life.

Clegg You ate the chicken.

Miranda (*caught out by this*) Yes, but I despise myself for it. If I was a better person I'd be a vegetarian.

Clegg I don't see anything wrong with it, but if you asked me to stop collecting butterflies, I'd do it. I'd do anything you asked me to.

Miranda Except let me fly away.

Clegg I'd rather not talk about that. It doesn't get us anywhere.

Miranda Anyway, I couldn't respect anyone, especially a man, if they did things just to please me. I'd want him to do them because he believed they were right. (*She gets up*) I want you to fix the bed. One of the legs is loose. (*She bends down to show him*) It's not a very good bed. Pretty cheap.

Clegg It wasn't. (*He goes over to look at it*)

Miranda Where did you buy it?

Clegg You know I can't tell you that.

Clegg bends down to look at the leg. Miranda moves out of the way and kicks him to the ground

Miranda runs out of the cellar into the outer cellar. She is heard banging on the outer cellar door and screaming, "Help! Help me, please!" etc.

Clegg gets up slowly, knowing she cannot escape. He waits for her to return

Miranda gives in and walks back into the cellar. She composes herself, turns and slaps him across the face. There is hatred in her eyes

Miranda How long are you going to keep me here?

Clegg I don't know. It depends.

Miranda On what? On my falling in love with you? Because if it does, I'll be here until I die. (*She turns and sits with her back to him*)

Clegg I don't expect you to understand me, I don't expect you to love me like most people. I just want you to try and understand me as much as you can and like me a little if you can.

Pause

I'll make a bargain. I'll tell you when you can leave — but only on certain conditions. My conditions are that you eat your food and you talk to me normally and don't try to escape like that again.

Miranda I can never agree to the last.

Clegg What about the first two?

Miranda You haven't said when.

Clegg In six weeks.

Miranda does not answer

Five weeks then.

Miranda I'll stay here a week and not a day longer.

Clegg I can't agree to that.

Miranda starts to weep silently, trying not to show it. Clegg goes to comfort her but she turns sharply, glaring at him

Please be reasonable. I've told you what you mean to me. Can't you see I haven't made all these arrangements just so you'd stay for a week? Look, look — I bought you all these clothes — your favourite colours — you haven't even tried any of them yet and all the work I had done on this place — it cost a fortune. I give you my word. When the time's up you can go as soon as you like.

Miranda I need a cigarette.

Clegg takes out a packet of cigarettes and a lighter from his jacket pocket. He passes them to Miranda who takes one and lights it

Two weeks.

Clegg You say two. I say five. I'll agree to a month. That'd be November the fourteenth.

Miranda Four weeks is November the eleventh.

Clegg I meant a calendar month, but make it twenty-eight days. I'll give you the odd three days.

Miranda Thank you very much.

Clegg hands Miranda a cup of coffee which she takes

I've got some conditions too. I can't live down here all the time. I must have some fresh air and light. And I must have a bath sometimes. I need drawing materials and music, a radio or a stereo or something, it's so quiet in here. And I need things from the chemist — you didn't think about that, did you?

Clegg What?

Miranda Never mind. I'll write a list. (*She drinks the coffee*) And I can't drink this. I only drink real coffee, you didn't know that little detail, did you? And I must have fresh fruit and salads, and get a cook book for God's sake. And I need some sort of exercise.

Clegg If I let you go outside, you'll escape.

Miranda (*sitting up quickly*) Do you know what "on parole" means?

Clegg I'm not stupid.

Miranda You could let me outside on parole. I'd promise not to shout or try to escape.

Clegg I'll think about it.

Miranda No! It's not too much to ask. If there really is no-one else about, it's no risk.

Clegg It's just you and me.

Miranda (*turning away*) Right, that's it. Keep me here as long as you like
but I won't say a word or eat a thing.
Clegg Of course you can have drawing materials. You only had to ask. And
a stereo — any music you want, books, anything like that. The same with
food, I'll get better with practice.
Miranda Fresh air?
Clegg It's too dangerous.

Pause

Well, perhaps at night. I'll see.
Miranda When?
Clegg I'll have to think about it. I'd have to tie you up.
Miranda But I'd be on parole.
Clegg Take it or leave it.
Miranda The bath?
Clegg (*looking around*) I suppose I could get a tub or something.
Miranda I want a proper bath. There must be one upstairs.
Clegg Well …
Miranda If I gave you my word, I wouldn't break it.
Clegg I'm sure.

The Lights change

Music

*Clegg brings on all the shopping and sets it up. There's a fruit bowl,
flowers, a stereo (no radio) and CDs, paper, pencils, brushes, paints etc.
He is obviously happy things are going better now. He also sets up a video
camera and tripod*

The Lights change

SCENE 4
THE BATH (DAY 5)

The cellar

Clegg is admiring Miranda's drawing

Clegg I've decided you can have a bath. I will allow it. But if you break your
promise you have to stay ——

Miranda I never break promises.
Clegg Will you give me your parole of honour then?
Miranda I give you my word of honour that I shall not try to escape.
Clegg Or signal?
Miranda Or signal.
Clegg (*taking a cord out of his pocket*) I'm going to tie you up.
Miranda But that's insulting.
Clegg I wouldn't blame you if you broke your word.

Miranda shrugs and holds her hands out, Clegg turns her round to tie them behind her then takes another cord to gag her

Miranda My wash things, and my towel.
Clegg Oh, yes. (*He gags her then collects her things. He selects a dress from the wardrobe then opens the cellar door*)

Miranda and Clegg exit through the cellar door

Lighting change

Clegg and Miranda enter DS. Miranda's relief to be outside is overwhelming. She stands still looking at the stars and breathing heavily. Clegg grips her tightly

The Lights change to reveal the rest of the house above and around the cellar. DS is a dining-room and lounge. The dining-room includes a table and chairs and a stereo with CDs. Stairs at either side of the stage lead up to a landing. Under the stairs is a cabinet with drawers filled with butterflies and photographs. On the landing, two doors lead to rooms including a bathroom

Clegg guides her up to the bathroom. He unties her hands and gag

There's no lock on the door, you can't even shut it, I've nailed a block in, but I shall respect your every privacy providing you keep your word. And don't bother screaming, there's no-one to hear you. I'll just be here.

Miranda goes into the bathroom

Clegg speaks through the door

I've thought a lot about bringing you up here, showing you the house, letting you see how I've had it done out. Maybe I am too strict. But I have to be. I can't take any risks. You do understand don't you?

(*Then more to himself*) You know, I used to think about you at work so much — make up stories where we met. I remember one went on for days. We met in a park where I had been collecting, you stopped and asked me all sorts of questions, you were fascinated. You said you wanted to draw some of the specimens so I went back with you. We had tea and a chat. You wanted to know so much, and then I sat there while you drew the catch. You loved it, you wanted to see my whole collection and draw it all. You said we'd never be apart again and you loved me, admired me and all I'd achieved.

Sometimes I think about us living here, just the two of us. You could have your own music room. You'd have the money to buy lots of paintings, cover all the walls with your own collection. People would come from miles away to see them. We'd have meetings here of the bug section and instead of saying nothing in case I made a mistake, we'd be the popular host and hostess. You, all pretty with your beautiful hair and pretty eyes, and of course, the other men green with envy.

Yes — that would be the best.

Miranda comes out changed into the new dress

Clegg is speechless at first

Miranda Thank you. You know it's funny, I suppose I should be shaking with fear. But I feel safe with you.
Clegg I'll never hurt you. Well ...
Miranda Unless I force you to, I know. (*She looks around mischievously*) Aren't you going to show me round the house?
Clegg It's late.
Miranda Please. How old is it?
Clegg There's a stone over the front door that's got "1621" on it.
Miranda So, it's probably quite old. Look at this. Did you choose these colours? And those pictures are disgusting.
Clegg (*wary of her movements*) They cost enough.
Miranda It's nothing to do with money. Can I look in here?

Miranda quickly darts off into another room

(*Off*) You're very neat and tidy.
Clegg This one's for Aunt Annie and Maggie when they come back from Australia.
Miranda (*off*) Are you sure they'll come back though? These pictures aren't bad.

Clegg I chose them.

Miranda enters from the room

Miranda (*as she enters*) Well, that's a surprise. They're all butterflies.

Miranda walks to the stairs. He follows her closely

What's down here?

She goes down the steps into the lounge, looking around, inspecting things

It's such a beautiful room. I can't believe you've put all this horrendous stuff in it.

Clegg looks offended

Come on, Frederick, look at it. Those wall lights — oh, no, you've got to be joking, look at those curtains. You can't do things like that to this beautiful room so many people have lived in. A house as old as this has a soul. Can't you see that?
Clegg I haven't any experience in furnishing.
Miranda You're hopeless. (*She walks over and tries the cabinet under the stairs*) What's in here?
Clegg Be careful, that's my collection.
Miranda Well, aren't you going to show me my fellow victims?
Clegg If you like.
Miranda I like.

Clegg enthusiastically opens a drawer of butterflies. Miranda is astonished by the obvious skill and patience that have gone into the collection

Did you buy them?
Clegg Of course not. All caught or bred by me and set and arranged by me. The lot. These are Chalkhill and Adonis Blues. There, you see that's a variation Ceroneus Adonis and those are variation Tithnus Chalkhills. They're better than anything at the Natural History Museum.
Miranda They're beautiful. But sad. (*She opens another drawer then another*) How many butterflies have you killed?
Clegg You can see.
Miranda Not just these. I'm thinking of all the butterflies that would have come from these if you hadn't killed them, all the beauty you've ended.
Clegg You can't tell.

Miranda You don't even share it. Who else sees these? You're like a miser, locking all this beauty away.

`Clegg (*disappointedly*) What difference do a few specimens make to a species?

Miranda (*ignoring him*) I hate people who collect things, and classify things, and give them names, and then forget all about them. That's what people are always doing in art. They call artists Post-Modernists or Impressionists or whatever and then put them in a drawer and don't see them as living individuals any more. It's against life, against everything.

Clegg I do photography as well. (*He closes the drawers and takes some photos from another drawer*) Here. They're not much. I haven't been doing it long.

Miranda They're dead. Not these particularly. All photos. When you draw something it lives and when you photograph it, it dies.

Clegg Well, I've never heard that before — they're a record.

Miranda Yes. Dead and dried up. But not bad, for photos.

Clegg I'd like to take some pictures of you.

Miranda Why?

Clegg You're what they call "photogenic". It would be a kind of souvenir — for when you're gone.

Miranda All right, if you want to. Tomorrow.

Clegg (*smiling*) Well, I think it's time you went back now.

Miranda Back in my drawer — OK.

Clegg leads Miranda back to the cellar

Lighting change

Did you get the Earl Grey?

Clegg (*confusedly*) Pardon?

Miranda The tea I asked for?

Clegg Oh, yes, and the Darjeeling.

Miranda May I have a cup?

Clegg Of course.

Clegg exits to the outer cellar

Miranda (*calling out*) Tell me more about your family.

Clegg (*off*) Nothing more to tell. That'd interest you.

Miranda That's not an answer.

Clegg Well, it's like I said ——

Miranda As I said.

Clegg enters

Clegg (*as he enters*) I used to be told I was good at English before I met you.
Miranda It doesn't matter. Tell me more about your father.
Clegg I told you. He was a sales representative for stationery and stuff.
Miranda A travelling salesman.
Clegg No, a sales representative. He got killed in a car crash. He was drunk. Aunt Annie says my mother drove him to drink. She was no good. (*He smiles*) Like me, I suppose.

Miranda is not impressed with his humour

She left my father for another man.
Miranda So you went to your aunt's.
Clegg Yes.
Miranda Like Mrs Joe and Pip.
Clegg Who?
Miranda Doesn't matter. What's she like?
Clegg All right.
Miranda And your cousin? You never talk about her.
Clegg Maggie? She's all right.
Miranda Well — tell me about her.
Clegg She's a cripple — spastic. She's real sharp and everything, always asking questions.
Miranda Can she walk?
Clegg A bit, but she's got a wheelchair.
Miranda Don't you feel sorry for her?
Clegg You have to be sorry for her, all the time, Aunt Annie makes sure of that. (*Thoughtfully*) Maggie makes everything around her deformed too. I can't explain. Like nobody else has any right to be normal. I mean, she doesn't complain outright. It's just the looks she gives, and you have to be dead careful. Suppose I say, not thinking, I nearly missed the bus this morning and I had to run like mad — Aunt Annie would say, "Think yourself lucky you *can* run". Maggie wouldn't say anything. She'd just look. You have to think very careful about what you say.
Miranda Carefully.
Clegg Carefully … Personally, I think spastics should be put out of their misery.
Miranda You don't mean that.
Clegg Why not? They don't have much point do they? Maggie just sits there.

Pause as Miranda does not know how to respond to this

Miranda Why didn't you move out?
Clegg I don't know.

Miranda Too much of a gentleman to leave two ladies on their own?
Clegg Too much of an idiot, more like.
Miranda And now they're in Australia spending all your money.
Clegg I suppose so.
Miranda Have you heard from them?
Clegg Yes, they write all the time. I got one this morning. (*He takes an envelope from his pocket*)
Miranda Can I read it? ... Go on, I'm interested.
Clegg I'll get the tea. (*He takes the letter out of the envelope and gives it to her*)

Clegg exits

Miranda opens the letter

Miranda (*reading*) "Dear Fred ..."
Clegg (*from outside*) She doesn't like "Frederick".
Miranda "Very pleased to have yours and, as I said in my last letter, it is your money. God has been very kind to you and you mustn't fly up in the face of his kindness. I notice you don't answer my question about the woman to clean. I know what men are and just remember what they say, cleanliness is next to godliness ... I am worried with all that money you won't lose your head, there are a lot of clever, dishonest people about these days. I brought you up as well as I could and if you do wrong it's the same as if I did it ... I worry about you so much ... When you do get a cleaner in, don't get one of the young ones they don't know how to clean properly nowadays."

Clegg returns with the tea which he puts on the table

Fuck! What a woman.
Clegg (*taken aback*) She wasn't educated properly.
Miranda It's so — petty.
Clegg She took me in. (*He takes the letter back*)
Miranda She certainly did, she's made a complete fool out of you.
Clegg Thank you very much.
Miranda Well, she has!
Clegg Oh, you're right as usual.
Miranda Don't start that again.
Clegg She never bossed me around half as much as you do.
Miranda I don't boss you around. I'm just trying to show you ——
Clegg Show me what?
Miranda Just show you how to be.
Clegg Show me how to be like you? You'll show me that and then leave me and I'll have no-one at all.

Miranda Oh, don't be so pathetic.

Clegg You just don't understand, do you? You've only got to walk into a room and people like you and want to be with you, you can talk to anyone about anything, I'm just —

Miranda Oh, shut up! Stop whinging! You're ugly enough already!

Silence

I'm sorry.

Clegg sits

Clegg (*about to pour the tea*) Shall I be mother?

Miranda groans at this and puts her head in her hands

What?

Miranda "Shall I be mother?"

Clegg What's wrong with that?

Miranda It's like those bloody pictures and curtains. It's — dead, stale, meaningless ... Don't you understand, can't you hear yourself saying it?

Clegg I think you'd better be mother then.

Miranda laughs at this then, realizing how inappropriate it is, suddenly turns away

I didn't mean to offend you.

Miranda (*quietly*) I just thought of my family. They won't be laughing over jolly cups of tea this evening.

Clegg Three weeks.

Miranda Don't remind me!

Clegg It's not that long.

Miranda I hate you. And you make me hate myself, you fucking bastard.

Clegg Don't swear, it's disgusting.

Miranda Bastard! You fucking little shithead! Wanker, pissing little son of a bitch. You — fucking bastard!

The Lights go down on Miranda

JUST LIKE A WOMAN

Clegg (*to the audience*) The thing that threw me most about Miranda was the way she spoke. You see I'd spent so much time with her in my head and

following her but I'd never actually heard her speak before we met so it was
a real shock. Still, she was just like a woman. Unpredictable. Nice one
minute and nasty the next. I don't hold it against her though. She probably
said and did some of those things just to show me she wasn't really refined
but she was. You only had to see how she held a cup or how she walked
to see how she was brought up. She wasn't stuck up like some of them but
it was there all the same. You could see it when she got sarcastic and
impatient with me because I couldn't explain myself or did things wrong.
She kept telling me, "stop thinking about class". That's just like a rich man
telling a poor man to stop thinking about money.

The Lights cross-fade to Miranda alone in the cellar writing on a pad of paper

HOW CAN HE LOVE ME?

Miranda (*to herself*) It's the seventh night. I keep thinking the same thing.
If only everyone knew. If only Mum, Dad, Minny and everyone knew. I
could share this fear then and not feel so alone. So I'm going to tell it now
to this pad. Try and set things down, keep calm.

Deep inside I get more and more frightened, but I can't show him. I mustn't.
I'm such a coward but I'm just glad to be alive. I don't want to die — I love
life so passionately, I never realized it before, I don't care what he does, as
long as I live.

Everything in my life was going so well — and now this — it's like falling
off the edge of the world. How can he love me? How can you love someone
you don't know? He wants to please me so much. He says this is the first
bad thing he's done — he's been saving up. But, I suppose, that's what
madmen must be like. I suppose, in the end, they're as shocked as everyone
else when they finally do something terrible. He must have been looking
for years for something to put his madness into. And now he's found me.

The Lights cross-fade back to Clegg. He has a camera

SHE SOON STOPPED SULKING

Clegg (*to the audience*) I agreed to a bath once a week. Each time I had to
screw the planks into the windows — I didn't like to leave them up. She
soon stopped sulking too, when she realized it did her no good. She began
to accept my rules and during the following week she let me spend a lot
more time with her.

SCENE 5
FIRST MENTION OF GEORGE (DAY 15)

The cellar

Music: Bach's Goldberg Variations

Miranda is drawing a portrait, we cannot see it. She is relaxed and seems quite content. Every now and then she closes her eyes to imagine the features of her subject. Clegg is taking photos of Miranda

Miranda You're lucky having no parents. Mine have only stayed together because of my sister and me.

Clegg Minny, isn't it?

Miranda (*with surprise*) Yes. My mother's a bitch. An ambitious, middle-class bitch. She drinks.

Clegg I know. Do you mind putting your hand up to your face for a bit, like this? (*He demonstrates a pose*)

Miranda Yes, I do mind. It looks ridiculous. My father said to me once, I don't know how two such bad parents could have produced two such good daughters. He was thinking of my sister really. She's the clever one.

Clegg You're clever too.

Miranda I'm a good draughtswoman. I might become a good artist, but I won't ever be a great one. I don't think so anyway.

Clegg You can't tell yet.

Miranda I'm not egocentric enough. I have to lean on something or someone. You want to lean on me. I can feel it. I expect it's your mother. You're probably looking for your mother.

Clegg I don't believe in all that stuff. I've never missed my mother.

Miranda We both want to lean.

Clegg You could lean on me financially.

Miranda And you on me for everything else? Fuck off.

Clegg stares at this, then takes another photo

No, that's enough. Just sit down, will you — I can't concentrate with you walking up and down.

Clegg (*moving behind Miranda to look at the drawing*) How's it coming along? (*He studies the drawing*) That's not me.

Miranda (*with surprise*) I know.

Clegg I thought you were drawing me. I thought that's why you wanted me to stay.

Miranda No, I just wanted some company.

Clegg Who is it? Anyone special?

Miranda Not really.
Clegg You don't know him then?
Miranda No, he doesn't exist. (*Tapping her head*) Only in here.

Pause

Clegg I know him.
Miranda (*laughing*) You can't.
Clegg I saw you go to his house once.

Caught out, Miranda is chilled by the thought of Clegg following her there

It's a good likeness. It is him, isn't it? Who is he? Your uncle or someone?
Miranda He's one of my teachers.
Clegg An art teacher?
Miranda Yes.
Clegg I've never seen him at your college.
Miranda No, he wouldn't go there.
Clegg So your parents pay all that money for that college with all those professors and you still need to go to another one after that. That doesn't make sense, Miranda.
Miranda (*trying to avoid the subject*) I got a scholarship, remember?
Clegg What?
Miranda (*thrown*) My parents don't pay any money for me to go to college.

They look at each other

He's a good friend, he's taught me a lot. I miss him, that's all. There are things you don't know about me. Things you've taken away from me — things you've taken me away from — unfinished things.
Clegg Between you and him?
Miranda Not just him.
Clegg That's disgusting. He must be over fifty.
Miranda It's not like that.
Clegg Then what is it like? Tell me.
Miranda He's ... I've learnt a lot from him. We have a very special friendship. He's had an incredible life.
Clegg Oh, yes, I know what sort of friendship he'd like to have with you. So, what does he teach you then? Why's he so special?
Miranda I can't sum it up just like that.
Clegg Try. That's what you're good at — words.

Pause as Miranda knows she must be careful

Miranda He makes me question myself.

Another pause as Clegg considers this

Clegg What's the point in that? ... Well?
Miranda I can't explain — he's had so much experience — he's seen so much, knows so much — and he says exactly what he thinks. I've never met anyone like him before.
Clegg I love you more than anyone else could, Miranda.
Miranda I know. Look, this is ridiculous, we're both going mad caged up in here. Couldn't we go for a quick walk?
Clegg It's wet outside.
Miranda (*struck by the thought of rain*) Is it? Come on — it'll do us both good. Just once round the garden, there'll be nobody about at this time of night. Please, Frederick?

She goes up to him and holds out her wrists. He gives in and ties her hands

Clegg leads Miranda out through the cellar door

Lighting change

Clegg and Miranda enter DS. *It is night and they walk, each in a different paradise. He holds her tight*

Smell the air — I never thought I would learn something from you, Mr Clegg, but you've really taught me the importance of air. Clean, fresh air.
Clegg (*very choked*) You wouldn't believe me if I told you I was very happy, would you? Because you don't think I feel things like you — deep down. I do, it's just I can't use words like you can. Just because you can't express your feelings it doesn't mean they're not deep. All I'm asking is that you understand how much I love you, how much I need you ...

Very near her now, he moves to kiss her, she screams and he puts his hand over her mouth. He pulls himself away from her

Do you want to walk some more?

Miranda, very shocked, shakes her head

They move back inside the cellar and Clegg unties her

Miranda I'd like my supper now, please. Please go and make it.

Clegg nods and turns to go

Wait ... I want to say something. It has to be said. You wanted to kiss me out there, didn't you?

Clegg (*embarrassed*) I'm sorry.

Miranda First of all, I want to thank you for not doing so — because I don't want you to kiss me. I realize I'm at your mercy. I realize I'm very lucky you're so decent about it.

Clegg (*not looking at her*) It won't happen again.

Miranda That's what I wanted to say. If it does happen again — and worse, and you have to give in to it, I want you to promise something.

Clegg It won't happen again.

Miranda Not to do it in a ... I mean don't knock me unconscious or chloroform me again or anything like that. I won't struggle, I'll let you do what you like.

Clegg It won't happen again. I forgot myself. I can't explain ...

Miranda The only thing is, if you ever do, I shall never respect you and I shall never, ever speak to you again. Do you understand? Now may I have my supper please.

Clegg, completely humiliated, turns and leaves

Black-out

SCENE 6
BACK FROM LONDON (DAY 18)

The cellar

Clegg knocks on the door of the cellar. He moves into the cellar and switches the light on. Miranda is nowhere to be seen

Clegg (*worried*) Miranda? ... Miranda?

Miranda (*from behind the screen*) Wait! Stay there!

Clegg What are you doing?

Miranda I'm on the toilet!

Clegg Oh, sorry. It's just the light was off.

Miranda (*to herself*) What do you think I'm doing — digging a bloody tunnel? (*She comes out spraying air freshener*) All right, come in.

Clegg moves into the cellar slowly

Yes, that's it — come along. Where have you been? You've been ages.

Clegg I've been to London.

Miranda I know, but you've been so long. You don't know what it's like to be locked in down here all day long on your own. It drives me mad.

Clegg But I was getting all the shopping.

Miranda I know, I know — I just got scared, that's all. I thought something might have happened to you. I thought you'd had a crash or something and I was going to be left down here forever. That's why I had the light off — I can't stand looking at these bloody walls.

Clegg I'm sorry. I had to go round so many different shops. The parking was terrible. It was pouring down in London. I got soaked through. (*He looks behind the screen*)

Miranda What are you doing?

Clegg I'm just checking.

Miranda For what? You are weird. Just come out of there.

Clegg (*coming out from behind the screen*) I'll get the shopping.

Miranda Yes ... Did you get everything?

Clegg exits

Clegg (*off*) Most of it.

Miranda Good.

Clegg returns with a box. He puts it on the table and begins to take out various items

Clegg Here we are. (*He takes out a bouquet of flowers*) These are for you.

Miranda Oh, thank you.

Clegg To brighten up the place.

Miranda They're lovely. I'll need a vase though. Can you get ...

Clegg (*taking out a vase*) Here.

Miranda Oh. Thought of everything.

Clegg takes out a box of chocolates

Again?

Clegg Just a treat.

Miranda Well, thank you.

Clegg Now, I hope this is all right. (*He takes out a large parcel*)

Miranda starts to unwrap it. It is an Eastern-style rug

It's not exactly the colours you asked for but they didn't have much to choose from.

Miranda throws the rug open and places it by the bed

Miranda It's perfect. Size isn't everything, but — it's really lovely. Was it expensive? ... Of course.

Clegg nods

What else? The music and books?
Clegg Yes — the compact discs. I managed to find most of them. (*He hands her more wrapped parcels*)
Miranda Why have you wrapped everything up?
Clegg It makes it nicer.

Miranda unwraps a CD

Miranda Is that why you're so late? You've been upstairs wrapping all these up while I've been down here worrying about you. Still it's very kind. Let me put this on. (*She puts the CD on*)

Music plays

Clegg takes more parcels of books out

Clegg I had to change too — I was so wet. It's been raining all day.
Miranda So you said.
Clegg I had to go to several different shops on the Charing Cross Road for these.

Miranda rips the parcels open

Miranda Excellent! It's just like Christmas!
Clegg That's what I thought.
Miranda Well, I'm sorry I didn't get you anything.
Clegg It doesn't matter.
Miranda I find it so difficult to get to the shops sometimes — you know.

Clegg does not laugh at this and Miranda is slightly embarrassed. She looks at the book

This is the one! Thank you.
Clegg And then there's these. (*He hands her a bag of toiletries*) I didn't bother wrapping them as they're for — practical use, you know.

Miranda takes out a large box of tampons

Miranda What did they say when you bought all these?
Clegg (*embarrassed*) I think they thought I was a bit peculiar.

Miranda laughs

Before you came it was even worse. I had to guess at your size.
Miranda (*thinking he means the tampons*) My size?
Clegg Yes, for the clothes.
Miranda Oh.
Clegg What?
Miranda Nothing. Go on.
Clegg So I had to ask this shop assistant who was about the same as you to try on all the clothes. It was very embarrassing. I'm very careful though. I never go to the same shop twice so no-one suspects. Somehow I think people know I live on my own. (*He sneezes*) I think I've caught a chill.
Miranda Well, you haven't dried your hair properly. My towel's over there. And get some water in that vase while I unwrap the rest.
Clegg I want to watch.
Miranda Well, it won't take that long — hurry. And then we'll have a cup of tea, all right?

Clegg exits

Clegg (*off*) I called into a couple of galleries with regards to that George Paston you were interested in.
Miranda (*to herself*) "With regards to". (*Out loud*) And?
Clegg Well, they'd all heard of him.
Miranda Of course they have — where did you go?
Clegg That place in Chelsea and the one in Hampstead.
Miranda What about Cork Street?
Clegg No, I didn't go there.
Miranda (*to herself*) Bloody hell! (*Out loud*) Why not? I told you to go there first. They can get his work so easily.

Clegg exits and returns with a large wrapped framed drawing

Miranda, taken aback, switches off the music

Is that his?
Clegg Yes.

Miranda takes the parcel off him

Miranda Can I open it?
Clegg Well, it wouldn't look much good on the wall like that.

Ignoring him, Miranda unwraps the frame. It is a drawing of a nude. Miranda sits on a chair

Miranda I don't know this.

She holds it up against the wall. They both look at it

Clegg Is it any good?

Miranda does not answer

It doesn't look finished to me — (*joking*) he hasn't coloured it in yet.

Miranda looks at him then back at the drawing

It's a bit rude, isn't it? I mean in an arty way, of course ... But — anyway it was the only one they had ... It was very expensive ... I had to carry it for miles — Miranda?
Miranda Look, thank you for all my presents. They're lovely. But I'd like to be alone now, do you mind?
Clegg (*hurt*) I thought you'd missed me?
Miranda What?
Clegg You said you didn't want to be on your own.
Miranda I know, I just — want to think for a while. I just need a bit of time, that's all. Come back later with supper.

Clegg exits, dejected

Miranda traces the lines on the drawing

You lost it with the hands, didn't you, George? This is old ... You must have been about my age when you did this. Who was she, George? Did you love her? Did you have to send her away because she "disturbed" you so much? ... "I like women, Miranda. I like the female form. I've met dozens of girls like you. Some I've known well, some I've slept with, two I've even married. Some I've hardly known at all, just seen them in a crowd, on a train — but you are a really strange one ... You'd be a bloody bore if you weren't so pretty." (*She kisses a line tenderly then she turns and sits on the bed still looking at the drawing*) It doesn't matter any more. When I get out things are going to be different, I promise you that ...

Miranda curls up on the bed

So very different.

Music as the Lights fade to ——

Black-out

ACT II
Scene 1
Appendicitis (Day 22)

The cellar

There are sounds of Miranda moaning in the darkness. This builds up until she is almost screaming

Clegg rushes in and turns the lights on in the cellar

Miranda is writhing on the bed in agony

Clegg Miranda? ... What's the matter?
Miranda (*weakly*) My stomach. It's going to burst.
Clegg What?
Miranda My appendix. Please, it hurts so much.
Clegg It might be something else.
Miranda Oh God — please get me a doctor.
Clegg I can't, you know that.
Miranda I'll promise you anything, please.
Clegg It'll be the end for me. You'll tell them.
Miranda I promise, I promise I won't tell them anything ... I need a doctor, Frederick.
Clegg I'll get you some tea. (*He turns*)
Miranda Oh please ... God, can't you see ... I'm going to die ...
Clegg I'll have to go down the lane — I don't have a telephone. I won't be long.
Miranda No — take me to a hospital. It's safer for you.
Clegg What's it matter, it's over, I'm finished.

Clegg rushes out leaving the cellar door open. Miranda waits a moment then gets up and runs out

The stage is empty. Sound of the outer cellar door slamming shut

Miranda walks back in slowly

Clegg comes in and starts to go about the usual morning routine of tidying up, cleaning the buckets out, etc. Miranda watches him, seething with anger and humiliation. From now on she becomes increasingly like a caged animal

Miranda Do something.
Clegg What?
Miranda Entertain me.
Clegg Well, what? Can I take some more photos?
Miranda *May* I. *May* I take some more photos. No you can't.
Clegg What then?
Miranda I don't know, anything. Sing, dance — anything.
Clegg I can't sing or dance.
Miranda Tell me a joke then.
Clegg I don't know any.
Miranda You must do. I thought it was obligatory for all men to know crude jokes.
Clegg I wouldn't tell you one even if I did.
Miranda Why not?
Clegg They're for men.
Miranda What do you think women talk about? I bet I know more dirty jokes than you do.
Clegg I wouldn't be surprised.
Miranda Oh, you're pathetic. (*She picks up the vase of flowers and throws it at him*) Here, catch!

The vase lands at his feet, the flowers go everywhere

Clegg (*shocked*) Don't do that, stop it!

She pulls a face at him

You should know better.
Miranda "You should know better".

Miranda starts to throw her clothes and books around the room

Clegg Miranda, don't, please — stop it.

Miranda makes a move to get past him, Clegg catches her

Miranda Let go! Don't touch me!

Clegg lets go of Miranda. She sits. Clegg starts to clear up

Leave it.

Clegg (*out of breath*) I'll just ——
Miranda No! I'll do it later.

Pause

It's your fault
Clegg I thought it might be.
Miranda Of course it is. What do you expect? Do you know you're the most perfect fucking specimen of petty narrow-mindedness I've ever met.
Clegg Am I?
Miranda Yes, you are. You hate people like me and my friends. You think we're stuck up with our "snobbish" voices and "snobbish" ways. You do, don't you? Yet, all you can put in our place is your pathetic refusal to have "nasty" thoughts or do "nasty" things. Do you know that every great thing in the history of art and every beautiful thing in life has been created by feelings that you would call "nasty". By passion, love, hatred, truth. Do you know that?
Clegg (*trying to avoid this new mood*) I don't know what you're talking about.
Miranda Yes, you do. Why do you keep on using those meaningless words — "nasty", "nice", "proper", "right"? Why are you so worried about what's *proper*? You're like a little old maid who thinks sex is dirty and everything except cups of weak tea in a stuffy old room is dirty. You take all the life out of life. You take the colour out of everything — words, this house, anything you touch. You kill it all. Why do you do that? Why?
Clegg I never had your advantages, that's why.
Miranda You could change. You're still young. You could learn. But no, what have you done? You've had a little dream, the sort of dream I suppose small boys have and wank about, and you fall over yourself to be nice to me. You buy me all these things trying to make me feel grateful and indebted to you so that you won't have to admit to yourself that the whole business of me being here is nasty, nasty, nasty! (*To herself*) This is useless.
Clegg I understand. I'm not educated.
Miranda (*exploding*) You're so fucking stupid! Listen to yourself — it's pathetic! Stop blaming everything on your background. It has nothing to do with that. This is about you, what you make out of your life. But all you ever do is complain and moan about what a tough time you've had. (*Laughing*) I mean you're a millionaire now, you could do whatever you liked. I can't believe it. Why you? Why did you have to win that money? It's so unfair. It's such a waste of all that money going to people like you who don't have a fucking clue how to use it.
Clegg What about the money that goes to charity?

Miranda (*with absolute contempt*) Oh, shut up. When you bought that ticket
were you thinking about your pound going to some good cause? That's
rubbish. It's greed, pure greed to get an easy passport through life. So you
don't have to struggle any more and make something of yourself. So you
can pack that bloody aunt of yours off, destroy the soul of a beautiful old
house and indulge in your sick fantasies about locking me up in a cellar.
So don't talk about some altruistic, charitable urge you felt that day. Think
of what you could do with that money, think of all the people struggling out
there, trying to express themselves — you could help them, instead of
massacring butterflies like a little schoolboy. You've got to use your life.
It's your choice.

*She catches herself lecturing him as she has been lectured so often by George
and she gives up*

Only you've got to start becoming a real human being first.
Clegg What do you mean?
Miranda If you have to ask, I can't give you the answer.

Clegg smiles at her nervously

And don't do that bloody smile!
Clegg There's not much else I can do. You're always right.
Miranda I don't want to be always right! Tell me I'm wrong!
Clegg But you're right — you know you are.
Miranda Oh, give me fucking strength! (*Suddenly, an exasperated scream*)
Aargh!
Clegg What's the matter?
Miranda You know, I never believed people like you really existed. I mean,
I must have stood next to you on the tube or passed you in the street, even
overheard you talking. But I never actually believed you existed — and
here you are driving me insane in this little world of yours! I'm going
completely fucking insane!

God help us ...

I always seem to end up by talking down to you. I hate it. It's you. You
always squirm one step lower than I can go.

Pause

I can't take this — if you can't see what's staring you in the face, it's not
my fault. Just go, get out.

Clegg exits

Miranda sits there in silence

BRILLIANT MIRANDA

Brilliant! Brilliant, Miranda, just fucking perfect! Go ahead, scold him like a little boy — that's really going to help, isn't it?

She gets out her notepad and starts to write

I've always thought I was more clever, cleverer than most. I've always thought I knew more, felt more, understood more. But I can't even handle Mr Frederick Clegg.

When I get out of here and he's caught I think I'll defend him. He needs all the help he can get and I'm the only person who could speak for him. He couldn't stand up in a court and speak for himself — he'd be useless. And his aunt would be even worse. I know I could never save him though — I'm his disease.

It's strange — in a way, part of me is glad this has happened. I think everyone should be locked up for a few weeks. I feel ... I feel older — and younger, both at the same time. I've learnt so much and I can see that most of me — was just not me — just things I'd picked up from other people. It's like being forced to scrape all that off ... All that mud from a stale life.

Clegg knocks on the door

SCENE 2
THE LETTER (DAY 22 continues)

The cellar. The same

Clegg (*off*) Miranda?
Miranda What?
Clegg (*off; hesitantly*) Can I come in?

Miranda quickly hides her notepad

Miranda Why?
Clegg (*off*) I want to ask you something.
Miranda Well, what is it?
Clegg (*off*) Errmm ... I've been thinking about what you said the other day and I was wondering if you still wanted to write that letter to your parents.
Miranda (*taken off guard*) Are you sure? Yes, yes, of course I do. Hang on a minute though ... I was just having a wash.
Clegg (*off*) Oh, all right.

Miranda runs over to the bedside table and takes out a small note hidden in the top of a perfume bottle and hides it in her pocket. She composes herself

Miranda OK — come in.

Clegg enters the cellar sheepishly

This is very good of you.

Clegg (*taking out a pen and paper from his jacket pocket*) Well, we'll do it now and I'll send it off in the morning.

Miranda All right. (*She takes the paper and goes over to the bed where she starts to write*)

Clegg "Dear Mum and Dad..."

Miranda looks up at him

Miranda (*attempting a joke*) Shouldn't I put the address first?

Miranda gives in to his dictation and starts writing

Clegg "I am safe and not in danger. Do not try and find me, it is impossible. I'm being well looked after — by a friend." Then put your name.

Miranda Is that all?

Clegg Yes. (*He hands her an envelope*) Here, you better address the envelope. Let me see the letter.

Miranda does so and, unnoticed by Clegg, slips the other smaller piece of paper from her pocket into the envelope. Clegg checks the letter and hands it back to her. Miranda seals the letter and gives it back to him

Miranda Thank you.

Clegg goes to leave, still fingering the envelope. He stops by the door and holds the letter up to the light. He feels it again, suspiciously, and rips it open and finds the hidden note

Clegg (*reading*) "Kidnapped by madman. Frederick Clegg — worked at Job Centre, won Lottery. Prisoner in cellar. Lonely, timbered cottage dated 1621. Hilly country, two hours from London. So far safe - ". (*Shocked and angry*) "Frightened"? But what have I done?

Miranda Nothing. That's why I'm frightened.

Clegg I don't understand.

Miranda (*looking down*) I'm waiting for you to do something.

Clegg I've promised and I'll promise again. You get all high and mighty because I don't take your word, I don't know why it's different for me.

Miranda I'm sorry.

Clegg I trusted you. I thought it would cheer you up, letting them know you're safe. Well, I'm not going to be used. (*He puts it in his pocket and turns away*)

Miranda (*softly*) Listen to me. I know I am safe here but you are keeping
me here by force. I admit it is quite a gentle force, but it is frightening.
Besides — you can't be a proper prisoner if you don't try to escape.

Clegg All you live for is the day you'll see the last of me. I'm still just a
nobody, aren't I?

Miranda I want to see the last of this place, not you.

Clegg And mad? Do you think a madman would have treated you the way
I have? I'll tell you what a madman would have done. He'd have killed you
by now. I suppose you think I'm going to go for you with a carving knife
or something. That's stupid — I mean how stupid can you get? All right,
you think I'm not normal keeping you here like this. You think I'm crazy
or something. Well, I can tell you there'd be a lot more of this kind of thing
if more people had the money and the time to do it. (*Pause*) Don't you
realize that? ... Eh?

Miranda What I fear in you is something you don't know is in you.

Clegg That's just talk — you just make up everything as you go along so I
can't understand it.

Miranda We all want things we can't have. Being a decent human being is
accepting that.

Clegg We all take what we can get. And if we haven't had much most of our
life we make up for it while the going is good. Of course you wouldn't
understand that, would you? (*He sits, on the verge of tears*) It could work.
It really could — if you just tried a bit. I've done so much for you. I've tried
so hard and you've done nothing in return. How can you say I'm mad?

Miranda (*smiling*) Not mad — I just think you need help.

Clegg The only help I need is for you to treat me properly!

Miranda I am, I am. Can't you see that? I just think you need help — to see
how I really am — not this person you think I am —- I think you've just built
me up too much, that's all.

Pause. They are both at a loss

Don't you feel this has gone on long enough?

Clegg One more week, that's all.

Miranda Why can't I go now?

Clegg You just can't.

Miranda I've done everything you want. What difference will another week
make?

Clegg does not answer

It's not fair, Frederick.

Clegg Life isn't fair.

Miranda Well, what do you want to happen in this last week then?

Clegg Nothing. Just not this.
Miranda But there must be something you want to do with me?
Clegg I just want to be with you.
Miranda In bed?
Clegg (*embarrassed*) No, I've told you.
Miranda But you do want to, don't you?
Clegg I don't want to talk about that.
Miranda Why not, if that's what you want?
Clegg I don't allow myself to think about what I know is wrong. I don't think it's right.
Miranda Oh, and this is right. You are unbelievable.
Clegg Thank you.
Miranda You know, if you do let me go, I definitely would want to see you again because you fascinate me.
Clegg Like going to the zoo?
Miranda To try and understand you.
Clegg You'll never do that. (*He turns to go*)
Miranda No, I don't think I ever will. (*Calling him back*) Will you send the letter?

Clegg stops

Clegg I'll think about it.
Miranda Please. For me.
Clegg Very well.

The Lights fade on Miranda as Clegg moves DS *and tears up the letter*

THE FATAL DAY

I lived from day to day really, not thinking about the four weeks being up. I just thought there would be some arguing and she'd sulk and I'd get her to stay another month — or maybe more. Besides, those evenings we spent together — it was like we were the only people in the world. It's very difficult to explain, I don't think anyone would understand how happy we were then — I know Miranda was happy too — she wouldn't admit it, of course, but when you get to know someone that well you can just tell. Everyone has bad patches, that's all it was.

The Lights come up on the dining-room area. During the next section, he prepares for the dinner to come

After that night she didn't stop going on about leaving. She kept on saying that she would never tell a soul, and of course I had to say I believed her, but I knew even if she meant it the police or her parents would get it out of her in the end. And she kept on about how we would be friends and she'd help me choose pictures and introduce me to people.

At last the fatal day came. She suggested we had a celebration dinner upstairs. She gave me a list of things to buy and got very excited. I suppose I got excited too. Even then I felt what she felt. I even said I'd buy her a new dress for the occasion. So she drew me the exact style she wanted and gave me her exact measurements.

He puts a chloroform pad in his pocket

Naturally, my thoughts were far from happy that day. I don't know what I thought would happen. I hadn't been feeling well either with my cold.

I went into town and managed to get all the shopping plus something to surprise her later.

He puts a jewellery-box into a napkin

Music. The Lights change

SCENE 3
THE DINNER AND THE SEDUCTION (DAY 27)

Dining-room

The table is set for dinner. This includes a bottle of wine and glasses and a metal vase

Miranda enters. She has changed into the dress Clegg has bought for her. Her hair is up and she has make-up on. She looks like a different person. She is bright and happy — this is her last day. There is a smell of perfume in the air

Throughout this scene Clegg watches Miranda's every move

Miranda Well? (*She turns round and walks up and down in front of Clegg*)
Clegg (*stunned*) Very nice.
Miranda Is that all?
Clegg Beautiful.
Miranda I think what you are doing today, and tomorrow, is going to be one of the best things you've ever done.

Clegg One of the saddest.
Miranda No, it's not. I'm very proud of you. (*She looks at the table*) It's nice.
Clegg I thought that word meant nothing.
Miranda Some things are nice. May I have a drink?

Clegg pours her a glass from the bottle of wine. Miranda looks around and starts waving at imaginary people, as though in a restaurant

Hello, how are you? ... Oh good, this is my friend Frederick — we're out celebrating tonight ... It's a new start for the both of us ... (*To someone else*) Hello there, haven't seen you for weeks ... Where have I been? Oh well, you see this man kidnapped me and ... (*To Clegg*) Only joking. Come on, let's have some music. (*She goes over to the stereo*) Let's see — these are the same as mine downstairs. (*She puts on a CD*)

Gentle music begins to play

(*To an imaginary waiter*) Oh, this is our table. Thank you, you're so kind. Come on, Frederick, thank Jean-Pierre, he has reserved us our usual table.

Pause

Clegg (*shyly*) Thank you ... Jean-Pierre.

Miranda laughs. They both sit. Miranda takes up the napkin and finds the box

Miranda Is this for me?
Clegg Look and see.

Miranda opens the leather case and, amazed, stares at the diamond necklace inside

Miranda (*incredulous*) Are they real?
Clegg Of course. Only little stones but good quality.
Miranda They're beautiful. (*She has never been given anything like this before. She holds out the box*) I can't take them. I understand why you've given them to me, and I appreciate it very much, but — I can't take them.
Clegg I want you to have them. Please.
Miranda I'll wear them tonight. I'll pretend they're mine.
Clegg They are yours.
Miranda Put them on for me then. If you give a girl jewellery, you must put it on yourself.

Clegg walks round and, nervously, puts the necklace on Miranda. He sits back down

Do they suit me?

Clegg nods

I want to see. (*She gets up and walks to a mirror*)

Clegg gets up quickly too, watching her

Can't you trust me?
Clegg Yes, it's not that.
Miranda What is it then?
Clegg It's just — if you escaped now, you could still say I imprisoned you.
But if I take you home, I can say I released you — I know it's silly.
Miranda Here, sit down. (*She sits*)
Clegg Supper's ready. I'll go and get it ...
Miranda No, wait, I want to talk a bit first. Do you mind?

Clegg shakes his head and sits

What are you going to do when I've gone?
Clegg I haven't thought about it.
Miranda You'll keep in touch, won't you? Tell me how you're getting on?
Clegg If you like.
Miranda I like. And you must come and visit me. We'll go to the theatre or
something. We'll have to go somewhere posh so I can wear this again.
Clegg You'd be ashamed of me with all your friends.
Miranda I've told you I won't, Frederick. I've got lots of friends and I'm
not ashamed of any of them. I'm proud of you — of us. We've come a long
way and there's no reason why we can't carry on in London. You'll see,
you'll be just fine. This is a whole new beginning for both of us. (*Raising
her glass*) Here, let's make a toast. To us, to friendship.
Clegg Marry me. Please.

Silence

Everything I've got is yours. I don't expect anything. You can do what you
like — study art, music and everything. I won't ask for anything, anything
from you, except to be my wife in name and live here with me. You can
have your own bedroom and lock it every night.
Miranda I can't marry you. Marriage means love.
Clegg I love you.
Miranda But ... I can't give anything back.
Clegg I don't want much.
Miranda I know you don't. You only want the way I look and speak and
move. But I have other things to give. And I can't give them to you because
I don't love you.

Clegg (*a dark change as he sits back glaring at her*) Well — that changes everything, doesn't it?
Miranda What do you mean?
Clegg You know what I mean.

As Miranda takes all this in, her world turns upside down

Miranda All right — I will marry you. I'll marry you as soon as you like.

Clegg laughs

Isn't that what you want?
Clegg I suppose you think I don't know you need witnesses and all.
Miranda What?
Clegg You think I can't see through all your soft talk.
Miranda Frederick ...
Clegg Don't you Frederick me.
Miranda You promised you'd let me go. You can't break your promise like that.
Clegg I can do what I like!

Miranda assesses this disaster and, shaking, desperately tries to compose herself

Miranda May I have another drink?
Clegg Help yourself.

Miranda does so and drinks, looking at Clegg — Dutch courage for a racing mind

Miranda I'm trying, Frederick. I really am trying. You've done a lot for me and I appreciate it. I do like you, very much. You've been a real gentleman to me — you've treated me so well. Surely you can see that marriage wouldn't work for us. You can see that, can't you? I know you can. And I know this has all got out of hand, but it's not your fault. I know you don't want to keep me locked up here really, do you? (*She walks round to Clegg and stands over him*)

Clegg looks wary

Now, I want to see you in London, I want to take you out and for us to do things together, have fun together. We do have fun here but you wait and see, it'll be so much better in London. And if you don't want to meet my friends then we'll go out on our own — just the two of us. But you have to believe me, you have to trust me, Frederick, that's the most important thing in any relationship.

Miranda crouches beside him and lifts his head to hers

   Trust me. (*She kisses him gently on the lips*) Put your arms round me.

Clegg does so, trembling

   Now kiss me.

Clegg kisses her head

   Not like that.
Clegg I don't want to.
Miranda You don't want to? Why not?
Clegg I might go too far.
Miranda So might I. I don't care. (*She kisses him again*) There. All right?
Clegg (*nervously*) Yes.
Miranda Kiss me then.

Clegg kisses her very tentatively and shifts in the chair

   What's wrong?
Clegg Nothing.

Miranda gets up and pulls him up too

Miranda Hold me.

They embrace, Miranda in despair and Clegg in panic

   Wait. Let's just have the firelight.

She lowers the lights

   Don't worry, I'm not going anywhere.
Clegg It doesn't feel right. You're only pretending.
Miranda Am I? We'll see.

Miranda moves to him. She kisses him. She takes off his jacket

Clegg Please — please.
Miranda It's all right. Trust me. (*She stands back and takes off her dress. She undoes her hair and moves back to him*)
Clegg No ... You don't understand. Please ...

Miranda starts to undo his tie and shirt

Miranda Ssshh. I want to feel you next to me. Take this off. (*She takes off his shirt and kisses him*)

Clegg No.

Miranda Frederick, kiss me.

Clegg No — You don't understand ... (*He pushes her away*) Stop! (*He starts to dress*)

Miranda What's wrong? (*Pause*) Please say something.

Clegg I can't. It's not right.

Miranda Don't you like me touching you? Frederick? It's nothing to be frightened of.

Clegg I'm not like other people.

Miranda That's all right. Nor am I. Look, to tell you the truth, I've never done this before either.

Clegg That's not true.

Miranda It is.

Clegg You've always got men around you.

Miranda But I've never slept with any of them.

Pause

Here, just hold me — we don't have to do anything. (*She reaches out to him*)

Clegg Don't touch me!

Miranda gives in and starts to put her dress back on

Miranda You should have stopped me earlier.

Clegg I tried ... I ...

Miranda We're further apart than ever now.

Clegg How can we be further apart? You hated me before.

Miranda I pity you. I pity you for what you are and I pity you for not seeing what I am.

Clegg Oh, I can see what you are. Don't you think I can't.

Miranda throws a drink in his face. Clegg, in his disgust and fury takes out the chloroform pad and lunges at her. They fight. It is violent and Miranda hits Clegg hard over the head with the metal vase. He stumbles and falls. For a moment Miranda stands ready to deliver a final blow, perhaps even to kill him as he tries to get up, slipping in and out of consciousness. But she cannot do it and as she hesitates Clegg catches her. The struggle continues until Clegg manages to smother her with the pad. Miranda passes out. Clegg backs away breathing hard

You're so stupid, plain stupid. You just don't understand, do you? It's all so simple really — there are lots of ways you could please me, Miranda — if you just tried a little. But you never want to, do you? It's just the having, that's enough for me, nothing needs doing. I never asked you for anything else.

He moves back to her and starts to touch her unconscious body. He starts to kiss her but breaks down crying. Then he pulls away

This is your fault, you started it. You've ruined it all, everything, changed it all around. You've killed all the romance — can't you understand? I can't respect you now. You've made yourself like any woman. (*Backing away*) This isn't my fault — it's not my fault!

Clegg gets her photos out of the drawer. He lays them out on the table. He is in a terrible state, manic with his head still bloody. He glares at the photos, undoes his trousers and tries to masturbate

Clegg I *can* do it ... I *can* do it. (*He gives up and sits, sobbing with humiliation*)

The Lights fade

SCENE 4
ANOTHER BARGAIN (DAY 28)

The cellar

The Lights come up on Miranda pacing up and down

Clegg comes in with a meal. His head is bandaged

Miranda I thought you were never going to come down.
Clegg I'm lucky not to be dead.
Miranda (*seeing his bandaged head*) Did you wash it?
Clegg Yes.
Miranda Did you put anything on it?
Clegg It's all right. Don't fuss.

Clegg puts the tray down

Miranda I want to talk to you. I've tried everything. I'm not going to eat again until you let me go.

Clegg Thanks for the warning.

Miranda Unless we come to an arrangement.

Clegg Well? I haven't heard it yet.

Miranda I'm prepared to accept that you won't let me go at once, but I'm not prepared to stay down here any longer. I want to be upstairs. I want daylight and some fresh air.

Clegg Just like that?

Miranda Yes. You could keep me in one of the bedrooms. You can board it up like the bathroom. But I must be upstairs.

Clegg What are people going to think with boarded-up windows all over the place?

Miranda I'd rather starve to death than stay down here. Chain me to a fucking wall! Anything, but let me have some fresh air and daylight. It's so damp down here, I've caught your bloody cold. I feel so shut in — so alone.

Clegg You have no idea what it's like to be alone.

Miranda What do you think I've been these last two months?

Pause

Well? I want to be upstairs, do you understand?

Clegg I'll think about it.

Miranda No! Now! Or I don't touch any food and that will be murder.

Clegg thinks

Clegg I have a condition.

Miranda Yes?

Clegg I've been thinking too. I'd like to take some photographs.

Miranda Again? But you've taken so many already.

Clegg Not the sort I mean. I want to take pictures of you like you were last night. And you've got to look as if you enjoy it. You've got to pose the way I tell you to. I have to protect myself.

Miranda You mean, I pose for sick photos so that if I escape I won't dare tell the police.

Clegg That's the idea. Not sick. Just photos you wouldn't want to be published. You know, arty ones.

Miranda No way.

Clegg I'm only asking you to do what you did without asking last night.

Miranda No, what I did then was wrong. I did it, I did it out of complete despair. This is different. It's vile.

Clegg I don't see the difference. You did it once. You can do it again.

Miranda (*with head in her hands*) God, God, this is a fucking madhouse.

Clegg Either you do it or you don't get out at all. No walking out there. No baths. No nothing. You took me in for a bit. But you've just got one idea — to get away from me. Make a fool of me and tell the police. You're no better than a common prostitute. I used to think you were different from the rest. But you're just the same. You'd do any disgusting thing to get what you want.

Miranda Stop it. Stop it!

Clegg I could get a lot more expert than you in London, anytime. And do what I liked.

Miranda You fucking filthy bastard!

Clegg That's it. Go on, that's just your language.

Miranda You're breaking every decent human law, every decent human thing.

Clegg Decent! You're the one who took your clothes off. You asked for it. Now you've got it.

Miranda Get out! (*She throws a book at him*) Get away from me!

The Lights change

I Was Paying Her Back

Clegg It's hard to explain but I felt so much better after that — happy even. I saw how weak I had been and now, by letting her stew in her own juices for a while — I didn't take her any supper — I was paying her back for all the things she said and thought about me.

The Lights cross-fade to Miranda

All Those Empty Lives

Miranda is writing in her diary. She is becoming very ill

Miranda Where is everyone? Why haven't they come for me? (*She breaks down*) I wish I was stronger, I wish I didn't want to see you all so much ... My head hurts ... I can't think straight, I can't sleep ... George ... George, I'm so tired. Minny, my beautiful, baby sister, I'm so frightened, Minny. Oh, Minny I want to hold you again — be small again, sleeping together — soft and warm. I'm sorry I've been so bad to you, so jealous, I'm sorry. And George, I'm sorry I could never be what you wanted, the woman you saw in me ... I could never ... Oh shit! It doesn't matter, Miranda, you stupid, fucking — stupid girl! It doesn't matter, because you are you now. And that's enough and you can take this — d'you hear, you self-piteous, little shit? D'you hear me? He's not going to win, all right? He's not going to win. No-one else is going to help you because you don't need any help. Because this is all there is, this pain and darkness. Everyone's in a fucking cellar and no-one's going to help anyone!

(*Pulling herself together*) I can't think like this ... It's weak ... So bloody weak. The worst thing is ... No-one will ever know what I've done, how much I put into last night, the effort of giving myself to him, risking everything, the humiliation. I won't give in, I won't let him beat me.

The Lights fade

SCENE 5
YOU'RE NOT A HUMAN BEING (DAY 29)

The cellar

Miranda is curled up in bed

Clegg enters the cellar without any food but with his camera

Clegg Well? If you think all this lying around is going to make me feel sorry for you, you're wrong.
Miranda You're not a human being.

Clegg moves further into the room

Clegg Suppose I just left you here. What would you do then?
Miranda Prison's too good for you. When I get out I won't go to the police. I'll come here and kill you myself.
Clegg You talk too much.
Miranda I'm sick. What would you do if I needed a doctor?
Clegg You've tried that one before, remember?
Miranda It hurts when I cough.
Clegg You forget you got it off me, it's only a cold.
Miranda It's not a cold!
Clegg Of course it's a cold. It serves you right — I got it in London doing all that shopping for you.
Miranda It's not a cold. It's this place, it's killing me.
Clegg I'm not listening to your lies any more.
Miranda I'm not lying.
Clegg Oh no, you've never lied in your life. Of course not.
Miranda Oh God, you're not a man.
Clegg Say that again.

Miranda I said you're not a man.
Clegg All right. You've forgotten who's in charge here. Get out of bed.
Miranda Don't come near me.

Clegg pulls the bedclothes off her. She fights him weakly but he pulls her on to the floor

Clegg Come on, stand up, stand up.

He picks her up, tries to make her stand. They fight, knocking over the bedside lamp

The Lights darken

You're not getting out of this now. I've let you get away with far too much so you've got to start doing things for me. (*He gets her standing and holds her by the hair*) I've had enough of this! Do you hear me? Most men would have had it ages ago. I'm going to teach you a lesson. About who's in charge. All right?

Miranda, very weak, nods her head in terror

Now stand still!

Clegg backs away and picks up the camera. He starts taking photos. Blinding flashes. Occasionally, he moves her himself and adjusts her dressing-gown to reveal more. Miranda stands there, shivering and breathing hard

Stand straight ... Turn to your left ... Keep your head up! Open the dressing-gown, go on! Push it off the shoulder ... More! ... That's it ... All the way to the floor ... Now open the top ... Go on open it ... Now turn around ... Turn around! ...

Frenetic sound, white flashes across a red wash as the photos are simultaneously projected on to the wall behind him. They are cold, headless shots

Black-out

Clegg exits

The Lights come up slowly

Miranda stands alone

I HATE GOD

Miranda (*slowly*) I hate God. I hate whatever made this world. I hate whatever made the human race, made men like him. Words are no good any more. It's more than hatred, more than despair. I hate beyond hate.

The Lights fade

SCENE 6
I DON'T WANT TO DIE (DAY 30)

The cellar

Miranda is in bed. She is very weak now

Clegg enters the cellar with a tray

Miranda Where have you been? You must get a doctor.
Clegg I've brought you some food and coffee. You'll feel better once you've eaten.
Miranda I can't breathe ... My chest ... I have to lie on my side. Please.
Clegg I got some of the pills I used for my cold. They're strong. Here, take some. And some of your sleeping pills. That'll help, come on.

Clegg helps her to take some with water but she vomits

Miranda Oh God — please. Do you think I'd talk to you if I wasn't very bad. After all you've done.
Clegg It's just flu. You must eat.
Miranda It's not flu. I've got pneumonia or something.
Clegg Look, you'll be all right.
Miranda Please wipe my face.

Clegg wipes her face with the napkin

Clegg I'll go now then. Eat something when you're ready.
Miranda Don't ... Wait ... You must listen ... You must listen to me ... (*She starts to weep*)

Clegg takes her in his arms and rocks her

Clegg It's all right. You'll be all right. Don't worry.

Eventually she calms down

Miranda Why did you leave me?

Clegg I didn't leave you.

Miranda You've been gone so long …

Clegg No, no, it's only been a few hours.

Miranda Will you do something for me?

Clegg What?

Miranda Will you stay down here with me and leave the door open for some air?

Clegg Of course.

He opens the door and switches off the light and goes back to sit with her. There is only the sunlight from the outer cellar coming through the door

Miranda's breathing is quite shallow

Miranda Oh my God …

Clegg What?

Miranda The sun …

Clegg Yes, it's still quite early.

Miranda I haven't seen the sun for so long … You see, look … (*She reaches out; breathing hard with the effort*)

Clegg Careful, come on.

Miranda But can't you see the difference … Can't you see … It's beautiful … (*Her breathing is hard*) I don't want to die. I must have penicillin or something.

Clegg It's all right. You're over the worse now. I promise if you're not better tomorrow — I'll go for the doctor.

Miranda What will you do if I die?

Clegg You can't die of flu. Don't be silly.

Miranda Would you go away? Would you tell anyone?

Clegg Come on, get some rest now.

Miranda No, you must promise me, you must let them know what happened.

Clegg I don't want to talk about this.

Miranda Promise you'll tell everyone.

Clegg But you're not going ——

Miranda Promise me.

Clegg I promise.

Miranda (*very weakly*) Thank you. (*She falls asleep*)

Clegg, distressed, comes away from her — he realizes she is seriously ill now

The Lights fade on Miranda

I Was Beaten

Clegg (*to the audience*) That night she managed to sleep for a while. I didn't know what I was doing half the time, and as usual I had no-one to turn to. First thing the next morning I went to the doctors. You see, I did go, I did want her to get better — but I hadn't slept. I was so tired and there were so many people there — everyone was looking at me. Then the doctor came out — he stared straight at me — no sympathy, just looked at me like I was dirt.

You see, it all came so unexpected. I mean I thought I was acting for the best and within my rights. I had no idea she was as bad as she was, I wanted her to live so much but I couldn't risk getting help. I was beaten.

The thing is, looking at all those people in the waiting-room made me realize Miranda was the only person in the world for me — despite all she'd done. I felt I could forgive her now for all the past.

The Lights come up on the cellar. Miranda is lying on the floor

Miranda (*delirious*) George ... George ...
Clegg It's me, Frederick.
Miranda I don't want to die, George. Help me ...
Clegg George isn't here, Miranda, it's me, I'm looking after you ...
Miranda George ...
Clegg No, it's me ... There's no George ... I'm going to get you better. I love you ... I still love you so very much ...

Miranda reaches to the light

Miranda (*barely audible*) I love you ... George ... George ... I love you.
Clegg No, no, no.
Miranda I love you, George.
Clegg Don't talk any more, Miranda, don't say any more.

Silence, just Miranda's shallow quick breathing

Miranda ...

She is too weak to answer

Miranda, how would you feel if I took you upstairs? Eh? Come on, I'm going to look after you up there and get you all well again, you'll see. I'll get the doctor in and he'll get you better and then we'll start again. You can live with me up there, just like you always wanted.

Clegg is moving now, checking outside the door and then coming back in to take her in his arms like a newly-wed bride — talking to her all the time. He is exhausted and confused

Just you wait and see, everything is going to be just fine — and you like the old place so much, don't you? It'll just be you and me. Like we've always wanted ... Just you and me.

Miranda has stopped breathing

Miranda? ... Miranda? ... Miranda?

Clegg looks at her in disbelief. He takes her to the bed and lays her down, holding her tight

There is a long silence

The Lights fade

The video image of Miranda looking healthy and happy starts up

I'M ON MY OWN AGAIN

The Lights come up on Clegg sitting in front of a video camera. We are back in the present and it should become evident now that his narration throughout has been his video confession. The box of her things is next to him

(*Straight to the camera*) I couldn't go down there for a while after it all happened. It took me three days to dig a hole for her, in the orchard. I thought I'd go mad the night I moved her. I couldn't stand looking at her so I had to go in with a blanket in front of me and I threw it over her. I got round the smell with a fumigator.

For a while I thought maybe it was my fault she did what she did — and lost my respect. I even thought maybe I should kill myself and be found with her. It would be like *Romeo and Juliet*. I'd use the sleeping pills and buy lots of flowers, put them everywhere so when the police found us they'd understand ... I would be out of it then — no more worries, no more hiding, no more things you want to be and won't ever be. Finished, the lot.

(*He takes Miranda's diary out of the box and looks back through it*) But then I found this. She never loved me and she only ever thought of herself — and that old man. So, I'm putting this tape with her things in the deed

box in the loft. It won't be opened till I'm dead. And whoever finds it —
you can see for yourselves. There are two sides to every story, just like Aunt
Annie says. I did everything I could and she asked for everything she got.

I do miss her though. After all that work, all that effort and money, I'm on
my own again … Well, that's it.

*He gets up, switches the camera off and takes out the cassette. He puts it in
the box with her things. He makes to leave then turns*

(*To the audience*) I know what you're thinking … I aimed too high.
Miranda didn't respect me enough. (*He surveys the audience*) I should
have chosen someone who could listen, someone who would understand
me. Someone I could teach. Still, I'll know better next time. That's the idea,
isn't it? To learn from our mistakes. In fact, I've already seen a girl who'd
be perfect as a guest, in a village not far from here. She isn't as pretty as
Miranda, of course, but she's the same size so the clothes would fit.
Anyway, it wouldn't be for love this time, just for … Well, the interest of
the thing … Yes … Just out of interest. (*He looks back at the cellar one
more time*) Tomorrow I'll go down and clear the place out proper. Put clean
sheets on the bed, give it a good airing — make it as good as new.

The Lights fade

THE END

FURNITURE AND PROPERTY LIST

ACT I
PROLOGUE

On stage: Shoe-box. *In it*: Scrapbook containing newspaper cuttings
Tray of supper including chicken and cup of coffee for **Clegg** in SCENE 2
Camera for **Clegg** in SCENE 4

THE CELLAR
Bed
Bedside table and lamp
Large folding screen. *Behind it*: bucket, air freshener
Wall mirror
Wardrobe. *In it*: clothes and underwear
Table and chair
Bookcase full of expensive art books

LOUNGE
Under stairs: Cabinet with drawers. *In it*: collection of butterflies;
   photographs
Stereo with CDs

DINING-ROOM
Table and chairs

SCENE 1

On stage: No additional props required

SCENE 2

On stage: No additional props required

Off stage: Shopping including fruit bowl, flowers, stereo (no radio), CDs, paper,
   notepad, pencils, brushes, paints (**Clegg**)
Video camera and tripod (**Clegg**)

Personal: **Clegg**: packet of cigarettes and lighter

SCENE 4

Set: **Miranda**'s drawing

Off stage: Tea (**Clegg**)

Personal: **Clegg**: 2 pieces of cord, envelope containing a letter

SCENE 5

On stage: No additional props required

SCENE 6

On stage: No additional props required

Off stage: Box containing bouquet of flowers, vase, box of chocolates, wrapped
                Eastern-style rug, wrapped CDs, wrapped books, Bag of toiletries
                containing large box of tampons (**Clegg**)
                Large wrapped framed drawing of a nude (**Clegg**)

ACT II
SCENE 1

Set: THE CELLAR
                On bedside table: perfume bottle with small note hidden in top

                DINING-ROOM
                Napkins
                Jewellery-box containing diamond necklace
                Metal vase
                Decanter of wine
                Wine-glasses
                Chloroform pad
                Mirror on wall for SCENE 2

Personal: **Miranda**: cigarettes and lighter
                Clegg: pen and paper, envelope in jacket pocket

SCENE 2

On stage: No additional props required

SCENE 3

On stage: No additional props required

Scene 4

Off stage: Tray with meal (**Clegg**)

Personal: **Clegg**: bandage on head

Scene 5

Strike: Tray with meal

Scene 6

Off stage: Tray with food, coffee, water, pills, napkins (**Clegg**)

During black-out on page 53

Set: Video camera with cassette, box of **Miranda**'s things including her notepad/diary

LIGHTING PLOT

Practical fittings required: bedside lamp

ACT I, Prologue

To open: Darkness

Cue 1	A video projection begins; when ready *Bring up lights on* **Clegg**	(Page 1)
Cue 2	**Clegg**: "My secret little world." *Bring up lights on cellar*	(Page 3)
Cue 3	**Clegg** switches on the bedside lamp *Bring up practical lamp*	(Page 3)

ACT I, Scene 1

To open: General interior lighting in cellar

Cue 4	**Miranda** sits in absolute horror *Fade to black-out*	(Page 5)

ACT I, Scene 2

To open: Darkness

Cue 5	Knocking on the cellar door, then sound of keys in the lock *Bring up lighting on* **Miranda** *in cellar*	(Page 5)
Cue 6	**Miranda**: "Please, Frederick." *Cross-fade to* **Clegg** DS	(Page 9)
Cue 7	**Clegg** moves into the cellar *Bring lights up to half-state on* **Miranda**	(Page 10)

ACT I, Scene 3

To open: General interior lighting in cellar

Cue 8	**Clegg**: "I'm sure." *Lighting change*	(Page 14)

ACT I, SCENE 4

To open: General interior lighting in cellar

Cue 9   **Clegg** and **Miranda** exit through the cellar door   (Page 15)
             Cross-fade to night-time exterior DS

Cue 10   **Clegg** grips **Miranda**   (Page 15)
             Cross-fade to house interior: stairs and landing,
             dining-room and lounge

Cue 11   **Clegg** leads **Miranda** back to the cellar   (Page 18)
             Cross-fade to cellar

Cue 12   **Miranda**: "You — fucking bastard!"   (Page 21)
             Cross-fade to focus on **Clegg**

Cue 13   **Clegg**: " ... stop thinking about money."   (Page 22)
             Cross-fade to **Miranda**

Cue 14   **Clegg**: "... now he's found me."   (Page 22)
             Cross-fade to **Clegg**

ACT I, SCENE 5

To open: General interior lighting in cellar

Cue 15   **Clegg** leads **Miranda** out through the cellar door   (Page 25)
             Cross-fade to night-time exterior DS

Cue 16   **Clegg** and **Miranda** move back inside the cellar   (Page 25)
             Cross-fade to cellar

Cue 17   **Clegg** leaves   (Page 25)
             Black-out

ACT I, SCENE 6

To open: Semi-darkness in cellar

Cue 18   **Clegg** switches on the light in the cellar   (Page 25)
             Brighten interior cellar lighting

Cue 19   **Miranda**: " So very different."   (Page 30)
             Fade to Black-out

ACT II, SCENE 1

To open: Semi-darkness in cellar

Cue 20   **Clegg** rushes in and turns the lights on in the cellar   (Page 31)
             Brighten interior cellar lighting

ACT II, SCENE 2

To open: general interior lighting in cellar

Cue 21   **Clegg**: "Very well."   (Page 38)
             Cross-fade to focus on **Clegg**

Cue 22   **Clegg**: "...that's all it was."   (Page 38)
             Bring up interior lighting on dining-room and cabinets

ACT II, SCENE 3

To open: general interior lighting on dining-room and cabinets, fireglow

Cue 23   **Miranda** lowers the lights   (Page 43)
             Darken lighting

Cue 24   **Clegg** sits sobbing with humiliation; when ready   (Page 45)
             Fade to Black-out

ACT II, SCENE 4

To open: General interior lighting in cellar

Cue 25   **Miranda**: "Get away from me!"   (Page 47)
             Cross-fade to focus on **Clegg**

Cue 26   **Clegg**: "... she said and thought about me."   (Page 47)
             Cross-fade to **Miranda**

Cue 27   **Miranda**: " ... I won't let him beat me."   (Page 48)
             Fade to black-out

ACT II, SCENE 5

To open: General interior lighting in cellar with bedside practical on

Cue 28   **Clegg** and **Miranda** fight knocking over the lamp   (Page 49)
             Cut practical lamp. Darken lighting

Cue 29	**Clegg**: " Turn around!..." Frenetic sound *White flashes across a red wash*	(Page 49)
Cue 30	Photos of **Miranda** projected. When ready *Black-out*	(Page 49)
Cue 31	**Clegg** exits *Bring up lighting slowly*	(Page 49)
Cue 32	**Miranda**: "I hate beyond hate." *Fade to black-out*	(Page 50)

ACT II, SCENE 6

To open: General interior lighting in cellar

Cue 33	**Clegg** switches of the light *Darken interior lighting, with sunlight through the door*	(Page 51)
Cue 34	**Clegg** moves away from **Miranda** *Cross-fade to focus on* **Clegg**	(Page 51)
Cue 35	**Clegg**: " ... for all the past." *Cross-fade to cellar*	(Page 52)
Cue 36	**Clegg** lays **Miranda** on the bed. Long silence *Fade to black-out*	(Page 53)
Cue 42	A video image of **Miranda** begins. When ready *Bring up lights on* **Clegg**	(Page 53)
Cue 43	**Clegg**: " ... make it as good as new." *Fade to black-out*	(Page 54)

EFFECTS PLOT

ACT I

Cue 1	To open the PROLOGUE *Music —Bach's* Goldberg Variations	(Page 1)
Cue 2	The video freeze frames on a close shot of **Miranda** *Fade music*	(Page 1)
Cue 3	**Clegg**: "I'm sure." *Music until the end of scene*	(Page 14)
Cue 4	To open Act I, SCENE 5 *Music: Bach's* Goldberg Variations	(Page 23)
Cue 5	**Miranda** puts a CD on *Music*	(Page 28)
Cue 6	**Miranda** switches off the music *Cut music*	(Page 29)
Cue 7	**Miranda**: " So very different." *Music to play out* Act I	(Page 30)

ACT II

Cue 8	**Clegg** puts the jewellery-box into a napkin *Music to play out* SCENE 1	(Page 39)
Cue 9	**Miranda** puts on a CD *Gentle music*	(Page 40)
Cue 10	**Clegg** picks up the camera and takes pictures *Blinding camera flashes with each photograph*	(Page 49)
Cue 11	**Clegg**: "Turn around! ..." *Frenetic sound*	(Page 49)

PROJECTION PLOT

ACT I

Cue 1   Bach's *Goldberg Variations* plays. When ready   (Page 1)
          A video film of **Miranda**. *See full description on page* 1

ACT II

Cue 2   **Clegg**: "Turn around!..." Frenetic sound   (Page 49)
          Photos of **Miranda** *projected on to a red wash*

Cue 3   **Clegg** lays **Miranda** on to the bed. Black-out   (Page 53)
          Video image of **Miranda** *looking healthy and happy*

Cue 4   **Clegg** switches off the camera   (Page 54)
          Cut film projection

MADE AND PRINTED IN GREAT BRITAIN BY
LATIMER TREND & COMPANY LTD PLYMOUTH
MADE IN ENGLAND